DIVIDED
WE
FELL

JOANNE BARD

Ordering Information:

Prime Seven Media
518 Landmann St.
Tomah City, WI 54660

Printed in the United States of America

TABLE OF CONTENTS

CHAPTER ONE

It was a scorching summer evening when the airplane landed in Sault Ste Marie, Ontario. As I walked down the ramp, I saw my father and a gentleman waiting for my arrival. I walked up to my dad, and we made small talk which was not unusual from earlier meetings in the past. Somethings never change. We're on our way to the hospital for me to meet with who would become my new mother. She had just lost a baby named Lucy. We sat and visited for a bit and started our journey to the place I would now call home. As I opened the door to hell, I saw my younger brother Ken standing there. We hugged and said hello. It had been four long years since I had seen him. To my right was this little girl who was introduced as Lily. I now had my first half-sister.

It was a two-bedroom apartment and all of us kids shared the same room. I was asked by my aunt to call when I arrived at my destination. As I explained my living arrangements she was saddened and said these words that still ring in my head, I never should have let you go. I told her everything was okay.

Ken and I would climb out the window to the roof at night to escape the turmoil running through our home like a knife cutting through butter. It was peaceful there, or we would walk down to the sea channel separating the Sault from Buffalo. We would watch the boats going by and just enjoy the little quiet before entering the storm again. Dad and mom both worked but money was always scary. Dad was back to the old ways spending money in the bar entertaining the woman while Rose stayed at home getting angrier by the moment. When dad finally arrived home and entered the bedroom it became a war zone. Rose yelled and my father lost control as always. I ran to the hallway as I saw my dad raise his hand to hit her. I begged him not to do it and he only looked at me and hit her right in the face. I saw her hit the floor and he was so enraged he just kept punching her repeatedly. I held my hands to my ears muffle the sound of her screaming. Oh, how I remember those sounds and a flash of the past came streaming across my mind. I'm back in the Lion's den.

Life for us seemed to pass slowly each day, it was like walking on eggshells, afraid to speak or do anything that could set him off on a rampage. Mornings would be our only escape from the life of hell, off to school for and great activities. Rose and I didn't have a relationship. She would've preferred I never arrived in her world. She would remind me how much she hated me because I reminded her of my late mom. Sickening knowing, she was an acquaintance of my mother and sat and had drinks with her, while sleeping with my father. That's unforgivable on so many levels. She now has become a part of the fault in my mom's passing. You are a despicable human being. The feelings I had were mutual nontheless. She would treat me like a slave. I did all the housework and every weekend while everyone else could go outside to play I was buffing hardwood floors on my hands and knees until they bled. Dusting, vacuuming and washing floors. I would now become the housekeeper instead of the daughter. She became my enemy.

Dad was staying away a lot more and drinking the money away. He would make my brother and I go out and hunt for soda bottles to buy a loaf of bread. Oh, how we hated him for that. It was not long before rent was a few months behind and we were moving. This would also become a part of our lives, two different schools in one year.

We found a larger house that had a huge attic where my brother and I would share. He on one side and me on the other. Dad straightened out for a little while but that wasn't about to remain. The drinking started again and now we had a new addition to the family. Our half-brother John was born. The beatings began again, and Rose would be sporting a new pair of sunglasses to hide the evidence of the late-night ronde Vo with a fist. Even with the hatred she had for me I still felt sorry for what she had endured. I thought we would become friends, but I was dreaming. You don't always get what you want in life and that was one of them.

As time went on, I would become responsible for all the housework and on weekends I would have to spend all my time learning how to curl my hair, which could be a reason I don't today. I hated standing there trying to put these stupid bobby pins in my head. Where is my childhood and why has she stolen it from me? I had no friends, and I would envy the other siblings out there living there life and she took mine. Because she hated me. Such a bitter woman, Guilty Conscience maybe somehow, I doubt it. She had no conscience or class for that matter. My younger brother on the other hand was the apple of her eye, please, He was intelligent and the abbott reader which was her cup of tea. Pathetic really. The worst part was he knew it and relished in it. He would torment me on a regular basis. He enjoyed it when she was angry with me. It got so bad that one day it was too much. She made the rule one day my brother would prepare our lunch and then I. He would borrow his friend's bicycle to beat me home so he could make the lunch and then complain I was not home in time so she would be angry with me. Two weeks I endured this treatment until one day I saw him with a smirk on his face as he is cooking and I saw red, I ran up and grabbed a knife as he ran into a doorway and as he gripped the wall, I saw the knife going into his back, not deep before I realized what I had done. I dropped the knife to the floor and just shook. I just couldn't believe how much mental anquish he had done to me over an extended period. My next thought was my dad is going to beat me bad for this one. To my surprise dad wasn't angry, and just simply said that he shouldn't have made me so angry. Wow! Great stabbing let's eat. My brother would continue to pick on me, but never pushed it too extreme again.

I remember one day I came home, and the bathroom was flooding. Our next-door neighbor came over and apparently saved the day. Before the words came out of my mouth, my father gave her my Brownie Outfit I held onto as one of my memories from my last home and now it was gone. It didn't matter what I treasured; it was never respected. If he worked for a living maybe, then I would still have it. He started drinking and rent became in arrears. My siblings and I were sent home from school for passing out in class from a lack of food. Supper would be a mustard sandwich, or as a treat one with ketchup. Our cereal was puffed wheat without milk or sugar. Oh, how we longed for potatoes or meat. To top it all off we're moving again. A new school, new friends, and hopefully a new beginning. Who was I kidding?

We were moving again, this time to Guelph, Ontario to live with his arch enemy, his deceased wife's mother. The woman whom he despised. The same woman I despised. It didn't take long before we moved into a fourplex home in an enclosed backyard where everyone joined and played baseball. Dad would pull pranks late at night and everyone seemed to get along. We had a man who thought he was Captain America dad would say. Things seemed good until one day someone broke a window. My brothers and I accused the next-door neighbor's child because frankly we didn't like him. Then we found out it was our little sister who did it. Dad called us one by one, and sucker punched us in the face. One time dad brought home a couple of friends from work, and they got into an intense argument. I wasn't feeling well so I was sleeping in my dad's room when I heard screaming and yelling. I ran to the doorway and asked dad what was happening, and he told me to close the door. As I did, I saw my dad smash this man's face into our stove. It was horrible, blood everywhere. Apparently, he accused my father of coming onto his wife. In all honesty he probably did.

Another incident happened when the woman behind us had her house on fire. My dad was the one who got there on time. He saved the day. It was in the papers, so I took the article to school for current events. I was so proud until I arrived home to find out my younger sister was the cause of the fire. We were forced to clean her place, do the laundry, and feed her family. My sister would endure a belt wrenching time. See she was used to it because she would get beaten every single day for wetting the bed. She would be black and blue and there were days I wished I could do the sheets just to stop her pain. It was gut wrenching to listen to her screams daily. My younger brother and I got caught stealing chocolate bars. Ken got away with it but not me. I was the oldest. He beat me across my back arms basically whenever it landed. He would yell at me to cry, but I just couldn't bow down and give him the satisfaction. When I think of this all I can say is, what were you thinking? I would look out the corner of my eye and there was the witch of the east with a smile on her face with every swing of the belt.

Then dad was jobless again, nothing unusual in that. We had no food and Rose would make these cookies that were hard as rock and absolutely no flavor. I would through them in my closet and starve before I would eat them. I guess this might explain my next criminal deed. There was a horse across the street in a field and I knew this girl loved horses, so stupid me sold her the horse on weekly payments. I knew it was wrong, but I did it anyway. Then I got caught. She went to my house and told my dad. Suddenly, I heard my name, and I knew the angry voice extremely well. I went into the house and was led to my bedroom where he told me to remove my shirt and struck me repeatedly with the same words demanding I cry and of course I wouldn't give him that pleasure. It might be the very reason I stayed tough all my life. It was my only defense. Sad but true nontheless. My punishment was to be locked in my room with a sandwich a day to live on for a week. Serve me right. Plus, I had to pay back every penny to the girl and apologize. Which I did. My parents made me see a psychiatrist after that and do all types of tests. Well at least it got me out of the house for a while.

One day my brother was told to wash down the stairs before they got home. Well Steve picked up the bucket and threw the water down the stairs and said there it is done. Well, that wasn't one of his brightest ideas and he got a punch in the face again. Dad had broken his nose. The boys would be told not to wrestle while they were gone to no avail. See they hated each other as said previously in my book, but it was the perfect opportunity for me to go from extremely poor to extraordinarily rich by telling them I would keep my mouth shut if they gave me their allowance. Great deal for me, not so much for them because they couldn't keep their paws off each other.

Then one day we were told that George was moving in. George is the son of my mom's mommy's dearest adoptions. She would have that poor boy beaten on a regular basis. He wasn't the smartest, but with what he had to endure his whole life it's no wonder. Little did we know he was a sleepwalker and a violent one at that. He would destroy a room in less than two minutes. One night he went into dad and Roses bedroom jumped on her and started punching her. After that, dad tied him to the bed, and I made him put a lock on my door. I was terrified. I felt so bad for George, it wasn't his fault. The adopted daughter Sarah, her precious daughter, was treated like a queen. Whatever she wanted she got. If she would've been a decent mother and treated her only daughter like that, she would have been in my life for a long time. Instead of cutting her life short.

There was another time when I had done something wrong, and dad beat me again. This time I ran away. It took several days before he found me at the woman's home he and I detested. The police came and picked me up to take me back home. I begged him not to take me there and showed him the belt welts on my back. The officer said he thought my dad was charming and would not hurt me again. As the officer was walking away, he told my father he better not hurt me again. The door slammed and I was pushed down a flight of stairs for sharing our family business with the police. All I could think about is how to escape this man who treated us like pounding boards instead of his children. What happened to him to turn him into this monster, and would it be enough for us to understand or be a little more understanding? Somehow, I doubt it.

It would always remain a part of our life so the silence of abuse mentally, physically and emotionally would just continue as the sun rose and fell in the evening. There would be no end to this nightmare we were living.

As the sun rose the next morning and as I peered out my window for a brighter and more rewarding day and made my way to the kitchen dad announced we were moving again. Probably behind on rent again. We were now on our way to London, Ontario. Larger than Guelph I believe and quite a distance. With so many moves in our lives long friendships were not a part of our life. Everyone was an acquaintance, no understanding of the word's devoted friends. So many hellos followed by short goodbyes. Non existing, just a part of our reality.

The house we moved into was a two-story old house that needed work. Dad agreed to strip the wallpaper and paint the house for a couple of months of free rent. Rose got a job working in a bank as dad through the money away on alcohol and ladies, anyone who would be entertained by his dry humor coming home at all hours of the night. One night Rose pushed his buttons, and the beating began. I got tired of saying anything, so I sat silently. Next morning the sunglasses appeared on her face once again. My older brother cracks off about it and dad warned him to shut his mouth, but no he continued vigorously and yelled at him you killed my mother. Without a moment in between, my father punched him square in the face, breaking a front tooth and a broken nose if not mistaken. I thought to myself, bro, what were you thinking? A sucker for punishment, are you insane? Rose would give birth to another half-brother named Charles. He was my favorite. I would take care of him and take him for buggy rides. Things remained tense as usual, and Christmas would come and go and never a present under the tree. We were used to it. One Christmas there was one. I bought it for Rose, my abuser, my enemy. Strange how that worked. It didn't change anything in our relationship.

Dad finally got a job and for once we thought our life would be back on track, wrong? Dad continued to stay in the bars after work and drink the money away. We would be starving. One night he arrived home at 4 am in the morning with ribs and all the trimmings. He woke us up and made us eat the food. We didn't seem to care, for we didn't know when the next meal would be. One night Dad and Rose went dressed to the nines as they were headed to the Christmas party at dad's workplace. The next morning dad arrived home after spending the night with a co-worker who was flaunting herself in front of him. A married woman, one with no class, a double home wreaker. When I asked where Rose was, he said in a mental facility for going crazy over the whole episode. Dad packed his things and left us all once again. It had only been four years and he was gone again. My brother Steve left with him. Finally,

Rose was released from the facility to come home and find him gone. How does it feel to have what you did to my mother come and do it to you? For me there was gratification. What made you think for a moment you were important to him? So once again we we were moving again, without dad.

Next destination was Kitchener, Ontario, back home where my whole life began and ended in tragedy. Five of us kids we moving on. We had an apartment, small, but Rose did her best. Our relationship worsened. She would make me sit at a table to write to my dad to tell him to get me out of there. Funny part I don't know where she was sending it, it's not like he left her a forwarding address. One day I met this guy named Brian and we started dating. Nothing serious of course. I was only 15 at the time. I said I was going to my friend's place. When I got there, we decided to visit him. Well, my brother was looking for me and said I had best return home at once. I walked in and she started screaming at me for not being in the apartment I said I was, she told me to go to my room and followed me with such hatred in her voice and eyes. She then hit me in the face, and I fought back punching her, meanwhile her friend was in the kitchen drinking tea. I Rose yelled out that I was a slut like my motherand I ran to the kitchen and grabbed a butcher knife while her words rang over and over in my head that I was a slut just like my mother. I told her you can call me a slut, but don't you ever call my mother one or I will kill you. Her friend ran from the apartment and called the police. It was going to be a long night for me.

When the officer's arrived they asked the woman if they could use the apartment to talk to me. She agreed. They sat me down and asked if I wanted to go back down and sort things out with her. My response was quick and simple with no thought process other than to say. You leave me here; she'll be dead by morning. It was already midnight when I was taken to my new residence. A group home is where I will be spending the rest of my teenage days. Once again, our siblings are divided and forever fallen. I would only see my younger brother once in four years.

CHAPTER TWO

My new home had 12 foster children, plus their own twin boys. They all seem to get along well, but I felt there was no place here for me. No abuse, but Strick rules and rules never really agreed with me completely. It was a month in, and I found myself in court alone waiting in a waiting room to hear my fate. My mind wondered if my father would appear, not likely, he was never there for me before. I was scared because I had never been in such a big place. Then I heard my name and was led into the courtroom. The Judge looked up and said hello and went straight to business. The words were hard to listen to as the judge asked if anyone was there to represent me, sadly no, it's just me. Then his mallet hit the desk and these words pounded in my head. You are now a ward of the courts until you're 21 years old. I was now an unwanted child, no one loved, missed, or wanted me. Oh, how I wanted to be 21 right now and just pass by this whole fiasco. I kept looking at the door praying this wasn't happening and if it is why? I didn't ask to be born, but there I was, in hell.

When I finally arrived back at the foster home there was cake and ice cream to celebrate. Celebrate what I thought? There's no celebration here, pain and suffering are all I felt. My stomach sickened with the uncertainty of my life. I'm living with strangers; my family is now gone. Will I ever see them again? After a few days I began to have nightmares and would wake up screaming. I would have this same dream over and over each night with no relief in sight. Mom would be on the top of a stairway as I watched my dad push her. She landed in a pool of blood at my feet, confusing me and my memories, playing games in my head. They sent me to a psychiatrist to help me sort it out. Eventually they stopped and life went on as it was. I would start to rebel, there were chores, nothing I was not use too growing up. Even though I chose this life to be away from the evil stepmother, it didn't mean it was the way I wanted things to be, but it was a reality.

It was the last day of school and all the schools got together for track and field. When I arrived, I was happy I would see my little brother. When I talked to his teacher, he said Ken stayed at the school because he wasn't feeling well. My teacher decided to take me to him. As I walked there, he was playing. I asked him why he didn't come today, and he hit me with news that tore my heart out. My Grandpa on my dad's side has passed away. I called him a liar as the tears rolled down my face. He was all I had left in this world. He can not be gone. My teacher drove me home and they were waiting to tell me. They confirmed my fears, he was gone. I told them I was going to the funeral home to see him, but was told that wasn't going to happen, I screamed at them and swore words I didn't even know I knew. So, they said they would contact my family to see if someone would swing by and take me. No one came. Two funerals that I never got to say goodbye to, mom and now grandpa. I still mourn them the most. I needed to say goodbye to move forward but instead was left in limbo hurting like it happened yesterday. I hated everyone for being so damn selfish and inconsiderate to my feelings and needs. I was family. Wasn't I? I threatened to go to see my grandpa when suddenly they grabbed me and locked me in a room so I couldn't leave. I hated them for taking that right away from me. I would remain in that room until morning. After that, nothing was the same between my foster parents and myself.

I started running away only to be brought back. I talked one girl into running away and she agreed. We headed for her mother's place in Oshawa, Ontario. We were there for about three days pierced our ears with ice and a sewing needle when there was a knock on the door. It was the police. I ran but Dolly didn't. They finally caught me and took us to the police department to wait for our foster parents to pick us up. The police tried to scare us by showing us the jail cells but as overconfident as I was, I laughed. He was a nice officer and bought us a steak dinner. Finally, our ride arrived and when I thought we were heading back I realized we were parked at the courthouse. I wasn't afraid, life taught me what's the point of that right? The judge threatened to admit me into a home for troubled teens where I would be confined. I didn't care at that point in my life, I've been through worse and survived, you cannot cause me anymore pain and heartache that I haven't already endured in my life. Where's the car judge take me now. The judge, however, was just making his threats. It was a long drive back in complete silence which was comforting to say the least. When we arrived, it was bedtime for us and no school.

My evil grandmother would visit so she could remind me how much she detested me. I felt the same way about her too, so water off a duck's back. I would run away for the last time. I was gone for a week. My foster mom called to tell me I am not welcome back into their home and my response was, I had no intention of returning to your house.

I would remain at the woman I hated for a week, but on the other hand I was with my little sister Lee. I was so happy to see her, but it was over in a flash when the phone rang, and my social worker was on the phone, she was taking me to another residence. It was a home with a partially disabled Mormon woman. I remember walking to the front door and ringing the bell. When this short woman opened the door. My social worker began to speak when I cut her off. I told her my name is Joanne, I come in when I want and go out when I want, you don't tell me what to do and we will get a long just fine. Where's my room? She pointed to the first room at the top of the stairs. I put my ear to the door to hear her reaction and was pleased when she said I was going to be trouble. My social worker said, no, she just needs someone to love her.

I would now meet the rest of the family. There was Theresa, a foster child, Coral their daughter, and twin boys Glen and Warren. Trevor,dad a physiologist and Josie a homemaker. Warren would sit there and give me google eyes. He had a little boy's first crush. Mom would tell him to stop, but that didn't work. Dad would teach drums and he was good. He taught me as well. I seemed to settle in quite nicely I might add, so nice that they broke their rule and allowed me to see some of my friends and boyfriend that Friday night. I was to return home at 10pm for a bath because mommy dearest was picking me up to see my sister for the weekend. I stumbled home at 2am drunker than a skunk. I remember mom asking me what time I call this, and my reply was any time you want to call it, I'm going to bed. I left for Guelph, Ontario the next morning knowing upon my return I was grounded for two weeks. I deserved it though. Things seemed good there and I was feeling like I fit in again with a feeling I lived and thrived for life, but I was lost along the way. Then one day we were shopping, and I found a coat I really loved. It was a little big, I didn't care, I wanted it. Theresa started to insult me, and I lost it and told her off and said to mind her own business and I didn't give a f.... what she thought. Mom yelled at me, and I screamed back at her and told her to shut her mouth. She is not my mother and will not tell me what to do. So homeward bound we were and nobody was talking to each , which felt like an extremely long drive back. When dad got home and heard the story, it was counselling time one on one. He took me into their bedroom to chat about it and asked me to tell my side as I did. I was punished by mom, and she Theresa was not, and I pleaded my case to have dad fix this. He in turn punished us both saying the two of us were in the wrong, her for provoking me to that point and me of course going to that point. I was happy, it was fair.

One day dad heard me playing guitar and singing and called me upstairs. He wanted to know if I wanted to sing in his band. I was thrilled for singing is my passion, so he took me to band practice, but nothing came from it. They played Jazz and I'm just a country girl, but it was flattering. We would go on these crazy road trip, and I would bring my guitar and sing. The boys just loved it. My life was feeling normal for the first time in years, then one day and looking back because I for the life of me can't remember what sparked this fight between mom and me. All I heard was my father was a cheat, he was not worth anything, a lousy father and I saw red. I told her she had no right to judge my father and to shut her filthy mouth, and then I heard her say go to your room your grounded. I came around the corner and I told her if she ever puts my father down again, I will leave a knife in her back and walk away. Of course, I didn't mean a word of it, but I wanted her to believe I would. Maybe I made her afraid of me so I wouldn't have to listen to that again. I know who my father is, and I certainly know what he is, and I did not need it spoon fed to me by her or anyone else. You're supposed to help me not criticize the life that was chosen for me. How dare she?

Once again, I found myself in dad's conference room, only this time I was going to control the conversation, she was not going to get away with her behavior. I told him what happened and that if she ever does that again I will leave a knife in her back. Dad was extremely upset, but didn't ground me, in fact he understood. Then it was mom's turn to enter dad's conference room. He reminded her they were there to help us kids to move on from our past, not to hinder our progress. I would find out decades later that dad slept at the bottom of the stairs for several nights so I wouldn't hurt his family. There would be only one more episode between mom and me, but not an angry one. I decided to try some drugs. LSD to be precise. I was high and freaking out on this drug, so Theresa went and tattletale me out and said I was high on drugs. Well, mom came into the room waddling like she does and all I could do was laugh and tell her she looked like a duck. I knew in the morning there would be consequences for my actions, but in that moment it did not much matter.

When I awoke that next morning mom ordered me to take a bath and to not lock the door. I did it without thinking and she started yelling at me to open it. I tried but the drugs were still in my system with there effect on me, so I struggled and finally opened it up. After my bath I sat in the living room as she lectured me and told me the police would be there shortly. What will I say, start a story now or you'll stumble, and they won't believe you. Then there was the knock on the door and in walked to the officers. Now running away as often as I had I was kind of used to dealing with them. I can do this. Then the questions started, where did I get the drug? Who sold it to me? What was it? Where did I buy it? All that came out of my mouth was I don't know; someone must have put it in my drink when I wasn't looking. I stuck with that story thick and thin. I wasn't a squealer. To my amazement the officer, after about an hour of me repeating the same story, believed me. Dodged a bullet. The matter was closed.

There was another time where I got myself into a pickle. This girl in my class in school didn't like what I had said to her and attacked me. Well, I wasn't going to allow her to punch me, so I fought back. In the meantime, the teacher and principal were outside the door when they heard the commotion they came running in. One of them grabbed her and one me. I struggled to get free and kick the principal in the shin. I was sent home and suspended for two weeks. When I arrived home mom was waiting, not at all angry. She asked what happened and I explained to her that the other girl started it, to my amazement mom got on the phone called the principal and demanded that the other girl get the same punishment as her daughter for starting the fight in the first place. The principal agreed. From that moment on, mom became my best friend. There was nothing I would not do for her. I would clean the house, the other girls in the home didn't appreciate my efforts. Hey, know if I did it, one day they would have to take my place. Then there was dad who every year on my birthday would repeat these same words as he kept getting closer and closer, many happy returns my dear. Then suddenly he would pick me up and toss me in the tub of water. Dad's birthday was the day before mine and the twin boys were the day after and me stuck in the middle. Dad and I had a wonderful relationship until one day I were trying to find out if my boyfriend was cheating on me, so I set a trap. Well, he found out and yelled at me and hung up. Dad decided to voice his opinion and I said a few words that struck him the wrong way. I insulted him and used language that would make a trucker turn red. I ran up the stairs from him as he followed behind me, he grabbed me, and I told him to never touch me again he was not my father. I got to my room when he burst in and saw the sadness in his eyes and told me he was sorry, and it broke his heart that this had happened between us because our relationship was solid. I could always count on him. I guess I lost a piece of his respect along with his heart. Nothing ever happened between us after that and for that I was grateful.

School was not going well for me. I spent most of my time in the vice principal's office. One time I took some valium from a kid in class and kind of took too many. Apparently, I said a few choice words to my teacher and was sent to the office again. Well. I got tired of waiting and left, they found me out in the football field laying down passed out. I was rushed to the hospital to have my stomach pumped and a scolding from mom. She was not angry, she was hurt, and it broke my heart knowing I was breaking hers. That was when, I had to realize, it's time to grow up and stop blaming the world and the people in it for your life.

I was at a turning point in my life, I was helping with the new foster girls coming in. I remember one day this one troubled young lady, so naive, started a fight with mom saying her dad would come to get her and make her life so wonderful again. Hogwash, you're a delusional little girl. Before I could think the words clearly in my head, I started to blurt out the words that had not only hurt me but haunted me at the same time, if your father wanted you, you wouldn't be here and with that I looked over to mom and went outside to have a smoke. As I was sitting there, I thought good for you, it hurt saying it knowing I was there once too, but a little acceptance took over. I think I was the one who was shell shocked by the words that trickled from my lips for the first time in my life. That's when I finally realized that all I had been doing was defending the monster who put me there. The one who sinned against his own children, who deserted us repeatedly. Who taught us not to be strong and successful, but to destroy our lives, our hopes, our dreams and become unimportant to him and society. I wanted so much more than this, to make a difference in the world, to be important, respected and loved. Funny, I thought that was supposed to come naturally, but have been shown differently in my world. It was not meant to be, I guess. When you come from the rubble, the stones can weigh heavily on you, some can lift it off, but others can be too weak and beaten down. The man I talk about, my father, doesn't deserve the satisfaction of my pain, he was the creator.

Life continued at the Ince family home, and I became the model daughter. It was a great turning point in my life. Time was good and the space I occupied was comfortable day by day. School was still an issue for I felt

I had to always keep my guard up, which always leads to trouble. A friend of mine during spring break decided to go to Electro home Canada and fill out an application. We weren't serious about it just messing around. We did a speed test with our hands and filled out the application and that was the end of it, so I thought.

On Monday morning I returned to school and was in my class when over the intercom I heard Joanne Schickler please come to the office. Everyone looked at me and my only response was I hadn't done anything wrong yet. I picked my books up and headed for the office. As I waited impatiently for him to call me in, I began sifting through my memory to see what I possibly did wrong this time, but nothing registered. Then I heard my name, I thought of running in the other direction, but it was too late. I walked in and waited to hear what he had to say.

He got right to the point. I got a call from Electro Home, and they want you to start work there as soon as possible. What? Electro Home? Why? Then he went ahead to say that the deal will be I will leave school with a passing grade. The principal agreed and it wasn't because he wanted to, but he really wanted me out of his school. I could sympathize with that. Then he asked what I wanted to do, and I said I will clean out my locker. I didn't enjoy school, that was obvious. I was embarking onto a different world now. I was 15 years old and heading for a full-time job on an assembly line. When I arrived home with the news, mom already knew. There was a rose on the table with a congratulations card attached. Tomorrow I will be up at 6am on the dot and heading towards a hopeful future. I arrived at the plant which was walking distance from home. My boss took me around the plant, and I was standing beside him as he was talking, and my world went dark. I woke up to him asking if I was okay as he was fanning me. I was so embarrassed. He told me to go home. I left disappointed knowing in less than ½ hour I was jobless and back in school. I was shattered, another failure to add to my life. When I walked through the door, mom smiled and said everything was fine, but please make sure when she comes to work to eat breakfast first for the chemicals can cause you to faint my boss told her. Yes! It was all good and I would return in the morning. I worked hard for two weeks to ref the profits with my first pay cheque. Wow! So much money. On top of my wage, which was rather high, I had extra for peace work. I was told by my boss my speed test with my hands was 99% and that is why they wanted me to work there. Mom and I made a deal, I would pay for room and board, but I would have to be home by 10pm every night. Sorry mom, but I don't think so. I stayed for quite a while and then found myself a one-bedroom apartment in an old house. It was lonely, but it was also peaceful too. My life was changing and for the better I thought.

CHAPTER THREE

As time went on, I was dating a guy named Joe Drury. My judgment in men was horrible. I seemed to attract the evil-minded ones, was it because it was all I knew growing up? It was all I seen and understood. It's how our father taught us. One day he told me if I didn't have sex with him, he would rape me. I was a virgin at the time, and scared, but not enough to remind him if he did touch me or came good on his threat, I will see him in jail for it. Then he grabbed me and raped me violently and laughed. I went to confide in mom who called the police, he was arrested and charged for my rape. He went to jail as I promised, but the psychological damage was done. Intimacy would become a major problem in my life after that, there would be fear when someone would want to be close to me in that way. I would need to work it through and find a solution to move forward or have it destroy me and any life I would want in the future. I would later find out the man who stole my innocence was a lifelong criminal, but at least I could take comfort in knowing he would go away for a long time. Did not change much for me, but the fear will eventually run its course. All things do happen to pass at some point.

I would go from one relationship to another to avoid intimacy problems arising until I met Dennis. The relationship didn't stand a chance for his demand for sex was too much for me to deal with, so I broke it off. Then I met Bill who was kind and gentle and started a relationship. I was still a ward of the courts, and I lost my job due to cutbacks, so I was homeless. He took me in. As our relationship grew, I decided to go on the pill. I wasn't ready for children in my life, but when I went, I found out I was pregnant with Dennis's child. I was 18 and going to have a child. Looked and felt like I was back on that roller coaster of poor judgement again. I could not have an abortion, or give the child up, so I made the biggest mistake of my life. I married Bill.

Three months if that, I asked for an annulment, that I had made the worst decision in my entire life other than dating Joe. Bill refused because he was in love with me, and I do not think I even knew the meaning of it. It would take me until 2022 to find the true meaning of love and you'll read about him in my third book. That's when I felt something wonderful, exciting, adventurous, wanting to be with him, kindness and understanding. What was it, I was feeling? It must be love because I have never felt it before. I knew it didn't exist in this marriage. This would be chalked down to failure again.

Nine months later and an extreme 38 hours (about 1 and a half days) of labor I found out that my son was a breach birth and deliverly finally happened by a surgeon, my son Stephen John Schram was born on June 12, 1973. Complications were there was a chance he would die, or I would, so I was left with the decision to choose. His life or mine and without hesitation I said mine. Little did I know, but Bill had to make the final decision because of my inability to think it through thoroughly. He chose the child; he would kill my son. The marriage was in shambles from that point on. I couldn't find it in my heart to forgive him for that. The only thing that ran through my head repeatedly was, It because he was not his child, so who cares. Newsflash, I did. He worked full-time as well as me. Him days and me nights so we wouldn't need a babysitter. We struggled to make ends meet and Bill would move from job to job. That was a major problem in the relationship. He disliked my family, and the feeling was mutual. My family never really became a family so through various stages in our life we would not talk to each other for years. How can you possibly be a family if you never were my philosophy. We could destroy each other with such hateful words. It was the Schickler temper to a degree of intending to inflict unnecessary pain on one another. Our enemies couldn't inflict that much pain and heartache on us, it was all we knew. Divided we fell, and we fell hard. Sadness was all we knew; nothing would ever change that.

As my marriage dragged on, the relationship soured, it always left me feeling empty inside. My life was not what I wanted or needed. Then the news came I was pregnant. All my siblings were having a child. Mommy dearest who continues to treat me like trash wouldn't believe me. I was very tiny and didn't really look much like a child was growing inside me. She walked up to me called me a liar, lifted my shirt to find out I wasn't lying after all. No apology of course. I was used to it. There was never a kind word coming out of her filthy mouth. She was an evil, wicked woman, and even today, I despised her so. We would all give birth to the children within two weeks apart. My beautiful daughter was born on July 19, 1975. My little princess was finally here. She came with medical problems though, but she was precious to me. She only

J O A N N E   B A R D

weighed 5LBS 4OZ but dropped below within hours and put into an incubator. Stephen weighed 10 lbs. 8 oz so it was a shell shock in size for sure. Shannon would go through milk allergy, stomach problems, jaundice, not to mention bronchitis pneumonia. She was hospitalized a lot.

She was extremely hyper, and I would be up for days without sleep, continuously crying for two weeks. I begged her father to stay home for one day so I could catch up in sleep, but he refused so I stumbled on sleepless until I had a nervous breakdown and asked the doctor to hospitalize me, and he refused. I left him with an ulternative that I have a full bottle of Tylenol # 3,I was left with no alternative but the doctor called Children's Aid Society to put her in care until I could get back on my feet again. My husband was furious and punched a hole in the wall. How mature. Nothing unusual in that considering all he had to do was help a little. After putting her into care I needed to attend counselling meetings on how to deal with your children. I didn't want to be there, but the choice was not mine. There I was sitting nervous when I locked eyes on this one woman. For some reason and I am not clear, I got up and went to sit beside her, threw out my name to her and she told me hers. It was Muriel Conn, and she would remain as my best friend for 47 years and counting. The sister I never had. We would go to each other's house once a week, her to mine and me to hers. We were family. I told her about my daughter and the circumstances behind it and let her know when Shannon was coming for a visit and it never failed, she would be sick with something every time. My friend would come to think there was something psychologically wrong, that I believed I had a child that didn't exist, and I desperately needed her friendship. Years later we would and still do which I am grateful, is laugh. The day did come through and I could prove I was not insane. She held her for the first time and in my heart, I believe the love for her was there and the very reason they are so close.

Muriel's marriage and mine were similar. Neither of us go anywhere in life other than stay-at-home spouses. Raising our children and wishing for brighter days to remove the fog in our lives so we can see clearly. We would all get together my highlite on weekends and Jim and Bill would get along. They should, they were a lot alike. I guess it went on for years, maybe seven years until finally I had had enough. Shannon was 18 months old when I finally kicked her father out. The fights, the cheating and the drinking was becoming too much. I needed a life so now I was on mother's allowance raising my children alone. It was better for all of us, peaceful and soon the same would follow with my friend. We still hung out once a week as we watched our children grow and become friends too. Their ages were so close Dayna and Stephen were the same age and Shannon and Shawn were. It was like it was meant to be and it was.

CHAPTER FOUR

As the months passed, I found myself in court with custody battles and maintenance charges which he only paid once. I got sole custody, and he had parental supervision for him to see the children. It was once a month. His parents would have to pick the children up and drop them off. I didn't trust the father alone with them and I guess the courts saw it the same way. I would only receive one months payment and then nothing. He now became exactly like my father, the man who didn't support his children in any aspects of life. My ex would still visit the children even though he did not pay for anything. No food or clothing, it was all left up to me. Sad really, I did not mind at all. The fighting was getting to be a ritual every night. It got to the point his presence would literally make my stomach turn. He was so childish, and I felt I was raising three children instead of two. He would stop by with other females to try and make me jealous, but it failed miserably. There wasn't love there to keep us together. He ran around with women and partied, but it didn't faze on me, I was beyond caring. My focus was on my children and helping them to cope with the major change in their life.

Steve started to rebel, and it was understandable, after all he had just lost his father. I knew and prayed he would make it through the changes. He was only four years old but old enough to feel the loss. The marriage was a, well let's just say it was not, a battle ground.

One night I was watching TV when I heard a familiar voice outside my daughter's window. It just happened to be my birthday. So, I decided to see who it was and sure enough it was my ex drunk, so drunk he was stumbling all over the place shooting his mouth off about my family. I went out there to shut him up and that is when I met a gentleman named Stuart. He was discussing my brother and sister and it was not the best of conversation. I introduced myself as their sister. I sat there for a while and then I left. It was two days later when Stuart came by to visit me, unsure of his intentions my safety guard came up in full force. My girlfriend stopped by to see if I could get a sitter and go out for a few drinks. He offered to babysit if I would buy him a case of beer. I happily agreed. I had not been out for an evening in seven long years, so I embraced it fully.

As we approached the bar and entered, I was pleasantly surprised to see my foster dad with his band. He became my protector for the evening. Dad was a big man who didn't tolerate nonsense from other people. He was God fearing but no one messed with his foster daughter. There was this one guy who I danced with just assumed I would be his for the night. Wrong plan for him. Dad told him to take his arm off me and to leave the bar at once or he would be escorted out. He finally agreed, a smart decision on his part. Don't get me wrong, my foster dad was a deeply religious man, a Mormon. I decided at that point just to go home. I was not used to the bar scene like my younger days not that I was old, 22. When I arrived home, we agreed that the babysitter would sleep on the couch because he lived way across town, and he had no vehicle either. Morning came and I fed him breakfast, thanked him for taking care of my children and off he went, with me thinking, I would probably never see him again. Well not quite.

CHAPTER FIVE

I t was a really sweltering day and as I was
busy with laundry, I received a surprise visit
from Stuart. We sat and talked for hours. My
daughter and him got along so well, in fact I
never saw her so content on his lap. I thought
how strange it was that she did not really
respond to her father in the same way. That
sure made me take notice. I mean every single
woman wants a man who will treat his chilren
as his own and that looked promising. He
would continue to come by and see how we
were making out and if we needed anything.

I really didn't know much about him.
He was two years younger, handsome, and
showed me respect before I even asked
for it. As we grew closer, I realized he was
a romantic, smooth with his words and
compliments that would melt any woman's

heart. Warning signs? Could very well be or he was just that kind of man. It wasn't long before I found out he lived with his parents and was unemployed. Between jobs or just not looking. We had been seeing each other for about a week when he moved in. I was excited, but also skeptical weighing the odds. He was so great to my daughter and my son, he seemed genuine. Only time will tell.

Then the time came for my best friend Muriel to meet him. She seemed to think he was all right, but something was itching at the back of her head. She is the type of woman that doesn't lead with her heart, common sense would bark through her brain, me on the other hand ran with my heart on my sleeve. Thinking back, I wished I had her steam and her courage. She didn't rush into a relationship like I foolishly did. She was stronger than I was in that department and many others. Our personalities were completely different, you could say day and night, but it worked, and we clicked. I could talk to her about anything, and I could trust her with my life. We did not always agree, but it never put a wedge between us. She was truly the sister I never really had and the sister I longed for. Can not say I blame my biological sister, we were separated all our life and honestly, I don't think we even knew how sisters were supposed to treat each other. Our future lives would be proof of that unfortunately. I still can not fathom any reasoning as to why my father would destroy our brother and sisterly love. Just like he destroyed our family twice. I guess you can not be a sister if you never were. How sad is that? Blood sometimes means absolutely nothing to some people. Do not get me wrong, it was not like we didn't try, we tried till we were blue in the face, but it never stuck long enough to get to know each other. We were strangers after all. Out of our control.

I would find out that the new man in my life knew my brother and sister quite well. He didn't like either one of them, which would be a problem for me in trying to build a relationship with my siblings. The feeling was mutual. As time went on Stuart and I were getting along when Bill re-entered my life with visiting rights. One day my daughter came back from her visit with a black eye and a cut lip. I was extremely angry and asked what he had done to her. She apparently fell down a flight of stairs. I didn't believe a word of it. Then suddenly, the guys were punching each other so I called the police as I was told by my lawyer. There was no need for macho attacks, especially in front of my daughter. Bill was put in the police car to calm down and Stuart was arrested on an old warrant. Either pay $50.00 or go to jail. He wasn't going to leave me with no funds so off to jail he went. Of course, I would be blamed for that in the future.

A few more weeks went by when he invited a couple over to our place for some drinks. Somewhere in the conversation an incident with my ex came up. Before I even had a chance to prepare myself, he grabbed me and threw me against the wall. I was 98 LBS soaking wet. That is when I found out he did drugs and alcohol. A lethal combination. Warning sign? Unfortunately, yes. I just brushed it off and put it out of my mind, at least for the time being. Things continued to get better, and we often visited Muriel. We both had sworn to each other that we would not allow anyone for any reason to come into our friendship. We kept that promise now for 47 years and growing....

As summer turned into winter, I had a few issues with my ex. He would sneak around my apartment building spying on me. Typical behavior from him. As mentioned earlier, he was immature. He would show up with other women to try and get a rise out of me, but it was pointless. There was no love, the flame that burned, oops! There was no love from the beginning, just a marriage of convivence, sadly, but a reality. There was never a question that he was in love with me, and this still is, but it was not a mutual feeling. His fault can not really be said.

One night, as I was watching TV my ex showed up peering into my apartment and Stuart had had enough and went out and chased him away. We decided it was time to move away.

We found ourselves a beautiful apartment in Waterloo, it was down the street from where he worked, convenient when you don't have a vehicle. The only problem was there was not a lot of shopping centers around that area, so I began to feel trapped. I had the children to keep me occupied so it was not too bad. I would also visit my friend every second week and her place. We would also get together at weekends. The ex would pop by with his mother every second weekend to pick the kids up and still no support payments for the children. It was pointless for me to even mention it anymore, it got tiring fast, so I just looked at him as I once looked at my father for never supporting his children when being raised by our relatives.

As time moved on, I would feel a shift in my new relationship. It happened when we decided to go out for a few drinks. While at the pub this gentleman asked him if he minded if I danced with him. He said he did not, so I obliged. When I returned to my seat in a fit of anger, he threw a drink in my face. Humiliated, I called a cab and went home. I decided the next morning I was getting myself into a relationship no greater than the last one. When he woke from the couch and apologized at once and assured me it wouldn't happen again. The fool in the corner, that is me, shrugged it off as usual.

In the meantime, I was dealing with a woman who despised my very existence, his mother Phillis Stickney. It started the first night I met her at their place. I brought my children with me. His father Harold took my son out to the garden to collect vegetables for dinner. During their conversation, my son accidentally called him grandpa. Harold found it amusing and adorable, but not his wife. She made it clear she didn't want her son with a woman going through a divorce with two children. She would almost resemble my mother's mommy dearest, no contest there, they were both winners. We remained civil with each of course, but deep down inside hate was brewing.

Things were starting to go downhill in my relationship with Stuart. We would argue a lot and he would control my entire world. Arguments especially while he was drinking. One night I just had enough, I found an apartment and I moved out. It was fantastic because I was just down the street from my best friend and sister Muriel. The apartment was quite a dump, but it was a fresh start and nothing, a little challenging work that can not cure that. Sadly, it was two days when he found me. Mr. romantic with flowers in his hand and an apology. He sat me down and without hesitation he asked me to marry him and put the diamond on my finger. In that moment and without thinking I said yes.

Thinking for me seems to have become a problem in my life. Evaluating my life would have been the most logical thing to do. We decided we couldn't live in that apartment and threatened to go to the health board. It got us out of the lease and into a two-bedroom basement apartment in a house right across from my friend's place. It was fantastic to be that close.

Then my friend got a job, and I became her full-time babysitter. I enjoyed spending time with Dayna and Shawn, they were like my own and close to the ages of my two. A little different though in the Behavioral department, for example, I decided to bake cake. When their mom came home after working the overnight shift, the little devils were rising. They made their way into the kitchen and, what I can only assume, they were hungry, took my cake and decided to not only decorate themselves but the entire kitchen too. Once, when visiting they both decided to check out what was in my purse.

We found my makeup all over the place and the evidence was all over them too. No sense in saying it was not me. It is funny but I don't remember seeing her ex- Jim coming around.

We were not at the house long before trouble started brewing in Stuart's and my relationship. He became controlling and demanded I have him adopt my children which I said no. He wanted to join the army, but also trap me in the relationship. One day things got out of control, and I sought refuge across the street at Muriel's home. A few minutes later he was there trying to kick her door in. She was terrified and I must admit I was too. She decided to just let him in. He finally calmed down and went back across the street. After that, things just got so bad I took the kids and left for St. Thomas where my ex was. We thought we would try it again, but that lasted maybe two weeks. There just was not love there. I also found out his mother was seeking custody of my children because she felt I was unfit due to the relationship I just left. I knew I had to leave and without thinking it through went straight back into the fire I left.

I decided I needed to discuss this with my son who was only four years old. I took him for a walk and told him I could not stay there any longer and that Shannon and I were leaving. I told him I wanted him to decide where he wanted to live. I realized before you criticize me, all my life people made choices for me in every situation possible, I couldn't force my child to follow me if his heart was not in it. He wanted to stay with his dad, so with my heart splitting in two, I said okay, not knowing the suffering I would go through because of that decision. I never forgot the words that quietly drippled off his tongue that he would not have a mother. I told him that I will always be his mother and nothing in this world would change that. I lost a part of my heart and soul that day. Strange, but true, it has never really healed.

It was a hot morning in St Thomas when Shannon and I took the bus to London and the train back to Kitchener, Ontario. Waiting for our arrival was the man I had just left. From the fire back to the frying pan. Mistake? I'm sure you will have your opinions. It was about three days later when I told my best friend in the world I was moving to Winnipeg, Manitoba. That was May 29, 1978, my mom's birthday. Now I knew I hated it there, but a fresh start was what I needed. We were off on an adventure by train to see my father who had absolutely no idea I was coming, and the worst part was I did not know if the address was the current. My father only kept in touch when it served his purposes.

I remember knocking on the door and this little girl answered. I asked who she was and if her daddy was around. She said her name was Sherri and she could not have been much older than my own daughter. We would find out they were a few months apart. Wonderful, adding another half-sister to my list. Brings the mixed breed at eight now. I would no find out for decades that I also had another half-sister named Kerri. Four different woman and nine children later, and not one did he support when he was absent of his significant role as dad!

It took a few minutes when finally, he appeared at the door and was surprised to see me. We talked for hours and of course he had to challenge me at cribbage to see who would buy supper. Looks like dad because I won all the games. Things were going well until one day with a few drinks in us all, my boyfriend walked up to my father and put him in a choke hold. A surprise attack and unfortunately in many ways. I was in shock, terrified that this was not going to end well. Dad told him to get out and told me that behavior from him will not be tolerated and I can leave with him too. It was about an hour later and everything was fine again, but I knew deep inside that the move on my father would last an eternity, I was right. A deep cut of complete disgust for each other, at least it was mutual. I knew then, we needed our own place, and as quickly as possible.

It was a week later when I managed to apply for a caretaking position in a large building. The rent was free and a small wage. Dad got Stuart a job with a friend roofing. Six months later we moved again to a smaller building for me, and he started working for City Parks Recreations. The wage was fantastic, but he wouldn't hold a job long. In the weeks ahead I was offered another job in an exceptionally large and beautiful building, so I took it. I would clean apartments to get my rent free, plus I cleaned one tower of the apartment building. It still didn't pay the bills, so I took another job as Head of the Housekeeping Department at a small motel. I was exhausted constantly going job to job when finally, I gave him an ultimatum to find employment or move out. What I can not wrap my head around is it was the perfect time to cut him from our lives. The heart on my sleeve had other plans.

It was about a week when he met me at work to tell me he got a job at The Wildwood

Country Club just down the street. He was upset it was only minimum wage and was prepared to reject the job, when I burst out the threat you either take it or don't bother coming back to the apartment I'm paying for. His better judgement won, smart choice. My choice in men needed upgrading. Two lazy men in less than 9 years. I had come to realize that this relationship was starting on the premise that it is not fitting, but better than being alone. Trust me and hear me when I say, it's better to be alone.

His problems stemmed from not only arrogance, but he was a bully, always wanting, to prove he was stronger and better than all men who crossed his path. He was charming though and extremely handsome, clinging, to his satisfaction of that asset. If there was a problem in the building, he was the first to arrive so he could fly in for the glory and rectify the problem and become the hero. Pathetic to have to spend your life trying to get people to notice you. His greatest attribute was a hopeless romantic. When he wanted to wine and dine you, it was spectacular, but it would only remain long enough for his own gratification, the bedroom was no different. As they say, his way or the highway, wish I took the time to reflect and taken the highway instead. The nights were long when it came to his sexual appetite, at least eight hours and seven days a week. I was walking around like a zombie with a lack of sleep. Something had to change.

I would get the pleasure of meeting the head of Security at the building. His name was Albert Crundwell, his wife Ollie and one young son Dave. Albert would become my mentor, relating on so many levels. We both had a problem working for other people. Our intellectual level was astonishing, and we realized that we perceived ourselves as being far more intelligent or only plain common sense would rule in. He would become my favorite supporter in anything I tried to carry out. He was also owner of a company called

Handi Helper which was extremely successful. This man has been in almost every profession that life had to offer. Before his passing I honestly believed his epitaph should say I wanted to be everything in life and succeeded. He would claim one more role as a Minister of his own church. Honesty was his forte and blunt was middle name. He would nickname me mouthy; competition was high when the two of us were in the same room. We held each other in highest regard with utmost respect for one another. I began to look at him increasingly like the father I never had. We stayed close until his time in this world ended and my heart was forever broken.

CHAPTER SIX

Albert Crundwell was a force to be reckoned with, former police officer among other traits and a no-nonsense kind of guy. As security of the two towers, he was a busy man. Close to the University the building was filled with students and some who loved to party. Some nights the excitement would begin, one night there was a wild party with people screaming, there was fighting in the hallway. All staff would have to attend as witnesses for each other. I was heading towards the commotion when I saw the head of security and his possies with bats in their hands heading directly into chaos. As I watched, that is when I saw my husband amongst the group. Heads were going to roll. This was Albert's building, and you abide by the rules. Little did anyone know; the party was being sponsored by a motorcycle gang. Wonderful. It was approximately 15 minutes into the fire when officers arrived at aid in bringing peace back into the building. I was in intrigued by this man and decided I would pay attention and watch him, maybe I can learn a few things from him. Let us just say he did not disappoint. An extremely intelligent man with the integrity of a lion. An extraordinarily successful business owner of several businesses. Yes, I think I will remain close to this spectacular man. There would always be the utmost respect for one another.

As time went on, I could sit for hours as he talked about his life and his business. I clung to his every word, fascinated by his knowledge in not only business, but law, one of my favorite subjects. He did as I said earlier, became my mentor and I could not have found a better person for the job. He would guide me through my career in Property Management. I succeeded because of his knowledge, life lessons and his own experience. Thank you, my friend. Thank you so much. You sir shall never be forgotten. I was honored to know this man and be a part of his life.

It would not take six months to turn Summerland in order with the security team we had. I would spend most of my life living in an apartment due to the nature of my job. It's difficult living in a building with so many different nationalities, and personalities. Did I enjoy living my life in the manner, honestly, no. It was like living in a prison with no escape. The only peace I got in my world was when I was sleeping, even then I would be woken up by a problem. If I had a choice to go back and remove that from my existence, well, I would in a heartbeat. My dream was to be a Prosecutor, but my past ended up dictating my future. Passed from home to home until the age of 18 and jumping into a loveless marriage was my destiny. Some can rise from tragedy and become better than they could imagine, and then there's me I guess could not. A stable home would no doubt have been a bonus, but it left me to feel selfless, unimportant even and most definitely unloved. If I could have allowed one moment's glance, just a tiny one to show me what my future would hold, it could have changed my entire world. I have the knowledge now, but just a little too late I'm afraid.

I speak of knowledge for it refers to making smarter choices in your life. The knowledge I needed the most was to find this marriage of love and happiness I had heard and seen glimpses of it in my life. Was there someone out there waiting for me, not a chance. So, I stayed in a marriage, a prison, if you will, not by a lot of physical abuse although there were times, but of emotional, psychological and sexual abuse. I lost my identity, my strengh, my humor, my personality. I became hardened. My staff would tell me I was two different people. One without a personality when he was around and a funny, intelligent and happy person when he was gone. I would be degraded constantly, several times told me how my contractors I hired for the building all wanted to was to bed me. They did not respect me. There was nothing I could find in my life I felt I carried out. I was surrounded by negativity and disrespect. Yet like a fool, I stayed, caged like a wounded animal.

Life went on and I did everything to concentrate on my daughter. She was my light when the world would go dark. My little princess. To this day, she does not truly know how much I love her. We had been through so much together. Everyone adored her. She was the cutest little girl in the world, yes, I am biased, but the fact is still she was loved instantly. Muriel would nickname her strawberry shortcake. My bosses loved her, along with Albert and Ollie, but something unknown to me for decades and my emphasis is on decades. Who were destroying my little girl inside every single day. Soon, something would take a huge piece of her away. Her heart and soul would be tortured. Lost forever. My heart breaks each day, and the confusion of why she withheld this from me for 35 long years, until recently. It has left me along with her broken. As years went on her brother became a faded memory, she was only eighteen months old when the separation took place, but he remained on my mind constantly. I only prayed he was healthy, happy and loved. It was not my intention to not be in contact with him, but I was never told his whereabouts. He knew, if he ever needed me, I would be there in a heartbeat or sooner. I never heard from my ex after that, and he certainly did not try and contact his daughter let alone send any support. I had accepted that a long time ago and decided he just was not worth the aggregation of dealing with his immaturity. Even today I wonder if Shannon even remembered him back then. He did not support and existence by his own choice. I could only see it as a terrible loss for him, she was a wonderful and beautiful little girl and a delight to know. Bias? Maybe? Someone must be.

CHAPTER SEVEN

It was not long before I found myself looking for another job. The one at Summerland ended because of personality clashes usually involving my husband. He walked and talked arrogance you could see the fumes around him. Tough guy, pushing the weaker aside. Belittling others. Those were the very people he kept in his circle, ones he could control as he did with his family. Far superior to everyone. Far more intelligent. The arrogance was so powerful that even decades later, my tolerance level is non existing. It is extremely difficult to communicate with someone who is so full of himself. It was now time to engage in heavy thinking on whether this is the way I want to spend the rest of my life. Unfortunately, and sad to admit, it was put on the back burner. We moved a few more times until I got a job working with someone who turned out to be a wonderful boss and a great friend. Gwen Terry. We got along famously; the boss you always wished you would not only work for but be friends as well. Her husband Jerry was both of our bosses. Just like his wife, he is a wonderful man. Gwen adored Shannon and the feeling was mutual. When I think back on it, I must honestly say, it was the best job I ever had in Property Management. I enjoyed my time there, but it would end like all good things do from time to time. The friendship remained and would grow.

Prior to making a move to another job with Winnipeg Regional Housing, I would make the second biggest mistake of my life. I agreed to marry Stuart. His mother hounded us about living the way we were. It never should have happened. When my poor judgement ended, always doing whatever everyone wants, the sacrifices became endless and happiness non existent, love a four-letter word. Gwen and

Jerry held the reception around their pool, and Albert walked me down the aisle, and my best friend Muriel came out to the wedding. Overall, that was fantastic, but why was I not happy? After everyone left, we moved into the townhouse. Things were good or as good as expected in the standards I was use too. After about a year it all came crumbling down. The behavior between Shannon and him started to evolve. I started to see my daughter's father's relationship a little strained. He would scold her a lot more than I had seen. Prior to working here. I worked afternoon-evening hours at the Wildwood Country club, and he worked days. This way we did not need a babysitter. I never saw them until weekends and even then, I would get called in. The relationship was working because we were never together. I was unaware if there were any problems at home, certainly if there were, I would have appreciated the opportunity to resolve the problem, but it remained locked up for many decades to come.

As I watched a little closer, I decided it was time to pack up my little girl and get out. I loaded the car and with the help of a male friend we left Manitoba in the dust. I was finally going home. Unfortunately, a few weeks the plan to stay was put on hold by my older Brother Steve. He wanted to go to Winnipeg, and conveniently I had the vehicle. I was going back to the place I had been trying to escape for years. Little did I know, my father was still in Winnipeg. We were always estranged for years, something he passed on to me. When we arrived, my brother knew exactly how to find him, and to find him we did. The reunion was about to begin. Here we all were staying at dad's tiny apartment. I had not seen him for years and the reunion was great. It was tight quarters, but it worked out. Steve was gone most of the time. This man had no problem having woman swarm over him. A look alike Michael Landon. Extremely handsome and profound sense of humor. He just had a way with the ladies, just like his dad.

We had a great relationship, only 11 months apart, I looked up to him. He was supporting Shannon and I while I waited for my Unemployment. It had been a long time and finally he said enough. He took me down there, walked up to the receptionist desk and demanded to talk to someone in charge. After his conversation we left and that day I looked at him differently. Now within a week I received my cheques. Thank your big brother. Shannon and her uccle had an extremely close relationship. He referred to her as his little princess and she adored him. Her love for him never faltered, the distance through the decades did not separate them and to this very day, it is like decades ago. That was her uncle steve. She loved him dearly. Then without warning our relationship shifted and the love I had for him I would question, I would pick him up from work at the Rib Shack where he was a cook, I was in the bar having a drink when his boss sat down to chat with me. Intrigued I listened to small talk when the conversation shifted to my vehicle. He wanted to know if my car was worth a certain amount of money because he was thinking of buying it. My older brother was about to sell my car from under me. My insides began to fuel, and I turned to him, and I informed him, it was my car, and it was not for sale. The relationship between him and I became zero, and void and I would not see him for years. The one who was my hero, became a villain. Over a lousy car. I have seen siblings hurting each other and I could only hang on to the hopes that my siblings would always be there for each other, not destroy each other. Is this our legacy, our father's doing, yes, absolutely. I thought the lost years we endured apart would make us want to finally be that family, but it was not to be. It never will, so instead we allow the pain, the hurt and confusion as to how we have become these strangers to our own blood destroy any chance. So, the sadness from the past just lingered slowly into our lives and turned to whatever love if there ever was any and drained it from our bodies. Let's chalk one up to daddy shall we. The bad seed in you has now festered in your children. Well done!

You hear that saying that trouble followed that poor boy, but he was the opposite, he followed trouble. My younger sister Lee once said that the only time our brother is on good behavior is when he is in jail, and we would laugh. Never a truer statement.

CHAPTER EIGHT

It was a sweltering summer day and I thought I would go for a drive and visit a good friend, Heather. As I was driving, I looked in my rear mirror and there was my ex-husband. I was stopped at a red light, so I had nowhere to go. He asked for me to go to the church parking lot so we could talk. Against my better judgement, I agreed. I knew deep down inside if I didn't, he would follow me until I did. Before I knew it, I was moved back in, like the Lion's den with my father. Common sense flew out the window and I was backed trapped in a horrible marriage. Once again, I climbed into a shell of a controlling man. What made me even contemplate on returning to the hell I just escaped. I was back to living my life under control. Once again stripped of my own personality to have one created by him. I seemed to be the creator of my own demise. It would take years to realize, I was the creator of my demise, but a woman trapped by constant stalking. Poems left on my car, constant phone calls, showing up unannounced. Jewelry sent to my office, there was no escape. The harassment was out of control and the only way to stop it was to return, return to an emptiness with nothing but sadness and abuse. To a place where I had to question who I was. I spent most of my life asking the very question.

It was time for me to find another Property Manager's job, I would go from one to another. A career chosen so I would be home or in the same building all the time. If given the choice of careers, I would not have chosen this. Once again, my entire life was dictated that way. I landed a job in a Highrise building this time. The pay was poor, but I did receive a free two bedroom. With a partner working, well I never wanted much, and my daughter was well supplied for, my number one priority.

Within a brief time, I noticed changes in my daughter's behavior. She started to steal rent money and ran away. I was destined to spend my weekends crying not knowing if my little girl was safe. I tried desperately to talk to her and try and understand why she was behaving in this manner; she would not speak to me.

I tried to continue when one day I received a call from the Children Aid Society (C.A.S.), they wanted to meet with my husband and me. They arrived at my place of employment, checked my daughter's living accommodations and we talked as to why she was with them. My head started to hurt as I was being told I had beaten my child because it was my birthday and she made pancakes, burned them and I lost control. I was speechless, I had never raised my hand to that girl, not because she did not need a tap upside the head from time to time, but as a beaten child myself, I knew it was hereditary and I was paranoid I would become my father. I was horrified to hear these accusations. The worst part was, I really disliked pancakes. I was told that after work the next day I was to show up and collect my daughter.

I remember sitting and waiting for my daughter to show, then she entered the room and the look on her face was uncomforting. The hate in her eyes. I looked at her and demanded to see the marks on her body from the beating I supposedly caused. I figured she owed me that much. Then there was silence for a moment when one worker spoke up and informed my daughter that there were children out there that seriously needed their help, but you are not one of them. You are going home. She started a tantrum, and it took four people to put her in my car. It did not do any good, she was gone the next day. The disruption to all our lives would cost me. I was let go from my job due to the constant problems with my daughter.

Once again out went the resumes and I ended up with another position with better company, higher pay and a beautiful townhouse. Things escalated with her, and my marriage was a disaster. The running away continued, the lies, and accusations started all over again. I was at my breaking point. I had no control over anything other than my job. I had to do the unforgivable. I had to put her in care. I took her to my job the next morning and as soon as their office opened, I found words I had no control over come from my lips. Those words have never been removed from my mind and probably never will. I informed the worker that I didn't care where you put her, just don't bring her back to my home. Never would I have imagined my child could bring me to say such words. It was just too much, missing person report every weekend, stealing, lies, bearing accusations, I was at my wits end. I spent decades trying to understand why she was doing this to me. What have I done so terribly wrong to make my child turn on me? I would find pictures of me ripped up. I just wanted, no I needed to know and try and understand, then I would at least have the power to fix what was so horribly broken. My little girl hated me, and I had absolutely no idea why and she was not forth coming helping me with the answers. My beautiful girl was gone.

Now it would be time to analyze this mess of a marriage. One day I arrived home from work, and he was sitting at the table waiting for me. As I walked up to the table, he through a police business card at me and told me to call, it's probably about my asshole daughter. I turned the card over and to my pleasant surprise, it was him they wanted. The pleasure of throwing it back at him was priceless as I told him it was him, they wanted. He went to the police station and was interrogated for sexual abuse of a child while we were separated. He got a lawyer, and he won. My escape from him just became my prison again.

I would spend time wondering how my life could end up with nothing but regret. It seemed since mom died my life was destined to turn to ruins. The past was creating my future into the same pattern. Nothing had changed, heartache after heartache, mistake after mistake and one troubled marriage to another. Why? There must be happiness and love out there somewhere for me, the problem was when, who and where? It was not for the lack of trying. When I think back now, I sacrificed my life for my children. I entered one loveless marriage for another so my children would be well supplied for. They were my priority and if I had to take less to give them more, there was no decision to be made. They say you will do anything for your children, I'm living proof of it. I thought I was making a good decision, but I hurt my children and myself staying in this relationship. My mistake was staying with him too long and jumping from relationship to another without coming up for air. Suffocating along with my kids. If I could have been given one wish in my lifetime, it would be to have become more than I was, better than I am and not afraid to carry on alone. To have the strength and the courage to become the person I always wanted to be. A successful career, my two beautiful children and a husband I could love until eternity. It was not meant to be.

CHAPTER NINE

My marriage was falling apart like thread on an old dress. Control, sexual, psychological and mental abuse was now a major concern to my mental state. I needed to get out. I could not breathe. I wanted to run out and cry. So, I packed up and left again. I was with this disaster of a marriage for eighteen years. I could not leave. He would hound me until the only recourse was to go back. To be honest and my best quality, our marriage was probably ten years for I had left so many times, I learned to pack all my personal stuff that I needed within thirty minutes. I guess his baby was good with goodbyes.

I wish I could say I stayed away, but I can not. The stalking started all over again and before I knew it. I was back. It took me a long time to decipher why I did not stay away.

Sadly, to say it would become the sole reason as being, I felt sorry for him. Yes, the worst reason to go back. Some would say it was because of my abusive past with my dad. It was all I was used to, and it was a lifetime reaction of poor taste in men. The next time would be better. I will take my time, not rush into another relationship. One can only hope.

My loveless marriage would continue for many years, and I would move on from job to job. I finally found another and to my surprise I was not asked to keep an apartment. It was the first time since I started my career. He was not happy because he hated my career and belittled me whenever he could. He would pick my staff for me. He wanted to control not only me, but every aspect of my life. He would insult me by saying all my tenants and contractors didn't appreciate my business skills, the. So, degrading and yet I tolerated it anyway.

He would spend every night drinking and doing drugs. I could not indulge because I felt one drunk idiot in the room was one too many, so I did not engage in his behavior. I knew I needed to escape for the last time. He was dragging me down. There were sleepless nights and fatigue was setting in. I was a mess. My staff would tell me how different I was when I was away from him over and over again to try and knock sense into me. Outgoing, funny, intelligent, but the minute Stuart would come into the room they said I buttoned up and would say nothing. I was two different people. Why could I not see that? Maybe because after eighteen years it became routine. It was not a relationship anymore and quite frankly I really can not understand what it was. I was heading towards disaster; I could not breathe anymore. I did not want to go home after work, I wanted to run and hide, I needed to get out. My life can not continue like this. I need to search for that woman who was once vibrant and now just a dime light. I need to find out who I am. I needed me, not this broken-down woman. The stalking must end this time and the connection severed completely. No more going backwards, it is time to leap into the future, find that life you have been desperately searching for, the love you never felt, the happiness that surrounded me but not within my reach. Does it really exist? Is there true love or just a myth, whatever the case may be, I need to know, see, and to feel. I want to feel alive!

In the weeks to follow, it became clear I needed to make my escape. I packed up my personal belongings and I moved out. The part that should have been thought through was moving in with another guy. Once again, I jumped from the frying pan into the fire. That pattern continues to control my life. It is a roller coaster ride that never ends. I did manage to change it a bit, my daughter came back into my life, so we got a place together. Unfortunately, it was short lived. Peter Coulombe is his name and he wanted me to move to British Columbia, Canada. I thought long and hard and decided to do exactly that.

I will never have to deal with Stuart and file for my divorce. He was no longer a part of my life and soon a faded memory of a life I swore to myself I would never live again.

Now, here I was wishing for a better future. Will this be my forever after? Time is of the essence. I was not by any means in love. I really did not know him, the last two mistakes I had made I at least knew, maybe that is why I thought it might work, but I knew deep down inside it was out of convenience, not love. There is that word again. How can it be four letters and hold so much meaning? My problem was experiencing it, capturing it and holding it close forever. Asking too much? Probably! My life has dictated love was a word with a hollow meaning, no substance, just a word. So, if by chance it happened, would I even know, that is the million-dollar question. Would I be able to welcome it, let alone understand it? I would sure like to try.

Peter and I said our goodbyes to our children and parents and were off to start a new life. Both recently separated from our spouses and making the distance further. Although my children told me to go, I was never sure if it was for my happiness or because our relationship was estranged, I would like to think it was the first statement, but I was not going to fool myself. I did not hear from my children much, strained yes. They had their lives and I had mine. Does not mean I liked it, I wanted more, but nagging question was, do they? Time will tell.

I got along with his family well, especially his mother. We were extremely close, and I adored her. In her eyes my children were accepted at once, and my grandchildren became Her's. She adored them all. I received the utmost respect in every way. She was an enormous influence in my life, and I treasured every moment we spent together until her passing. She was more my friend than a mother-in-law. We would talk for hours on the phone long distances, we never ran out of things to say. A remarkable woman and I was honored to have her in my life. She was the first after my mom to show me the meaning of love from a mother to a daughter. I lost that when I was seven, thinking I would never feel that again. I heard once that love was delayed pain. You eventually lose them, some quicker than others, to love turns to pain. It's just prolonged. They also say it's better to have been loved than to never have been loved before. My life has shown it has been the latter. I was willing to dive right in, either fail or succeed entirely, hoping for the latter.

Peter and I would marry three years later, and I was delighted when his mother attended the wedding and played a significant role in preparing the bride. I would think of my mother wishing she could share this moment, but it was not to be. That decision was made by her many decades before. My dad had never been to any of my weddings either. If you really must know, neither were my siblings. Strange to have a family, yet not have a family. They were absent from my life because we all chose that. It would not have taken a devastating amount of time to form a bond or at least start one. The battles in this family were destroying each other, sadly to say, the hurtful words that penetrated through us was not minor league, it was to rip the heart right out of you. To shatter you. When we unmask ourselves all we are, is monsters scared by our past ruining our futures. We cannot be siblings if we were never taught to love, care, understand, damn even feel something other than contempt for each other. The words coming from us innocent children of the past are heart wrenching enough you can feel the hate penetrating from their lips. Yes, dear old dad taught us well. It's sad to admit, we are not family, that is not what I have witnessed in other families. It is the cards we were dealt with, we just didn't get the winning hand.

I will go my entire life not ever understanding why life has turned us that way. I will not begin to understand the hatred inside and what brought it to our existence and after our father's death it would continue. Where is the blood relations? I would understand it better if we were not biological children, I would be able to put this to rest, but I will search my entire life looking and wondering why this has happened. Who am I kidding, I already know as told in Four Lost Children, our life has been dictated right from our very existence. It was our destiny, now I know what you are thinking, destiny can be what you make it, it is whether you have the tools and you know how to use them. A self help guide maybe? Anything would be acceptable and useful.

My other half siblings are different. They were allotted a second chance with new fathers and a mother who survived the abuse. They are still close, but biologically, the original four were not. Would not get another peak into the abyss. To relive the whole nightmare over and be passed on from home to home accept for one sister who shall remain nameless, for our relationship or lack of for a better word, is beyond repair. The hatred that burns inside our souls will not allow us to be anything other than enemies. I have dedicated too much time to trying to create our family that will never be, so acceptance and hopefully at least a little healing. The pain and sorrow, the confusion and lack of understanding will never go away. It is too evil and it has settled inside each one of us. The horrible part is bearing my soul and opening my heart has not changed a thing. It is all still the same. If I could find a way before my passing to find peace and harmony for our family, I would in a heartbeat I would erase it all, but when the damage has been done and believe me there is a lot of damage, it's time to discard it permanently. You can not salvage what someone else does not think is worth their time or effort. So, on we go pretending like each other does not exists. So terribly sad.

CHAPTER TEN

We left for British Columbia Canada in August of 1993. It was a beautiful day, and I knew the drive would be fantastic once we parted the Manitoba and Saskatchewan border. The prairies offer nothing but farmlands for scenery and long stretches of straight highway with no end in sight. Once you pass through there the world begins to look beautiful. The roads curve and you start to see the mountains. The animals on the side of the mountains socialize with each other. It was a magnificent view. The best part was it barely snowed there and after 40-50 below temperatures in Manitoba, that was music to my ears. There were also no mosquitoes which I have an allergy to.

Peter had a job already lined up through the last trucking company he worked for.

When we met, he was running a small firm, but moving to B.C. he would return as a driver. I tried to find work, but it was difficult at best. Prior to leaving Manitoba I was in an accident and the result was Fibromyalgia. It is a debilitating disease where you live in pain 24/7 with no release. I was medicated for sleep otherwise I would be up all night in pain. I would now have to learn by living a different lifestyle. I missed working. I would be in support groups and learning how to change my way of existing. With this disease everyone experiences the same pain, no one else's pain is stronger. What upset me the most was watching other patients use this to their advantage for pity to the point of putting themselves in a wheelchair. Me on the other hand was not going to accept my disability and take away my dignity. I was not about to have it control my life; experience has taught me that. I was going to fight it and to this day nothing has changed. Just needed to adjust a few things was all.

I would find myself in a ten-year battle fighting for compensation from this motor vehicle accident. The other driver is now deceased due to another accident solely his fault. He hit me 80 kilometers while I was stopped at a red light. I went flying into oncoming traffic, but luckily, they saw it all transpire in front of them. My life could have ended that very day. I guess God had another plan. I would not receive even a third of the lawsuit, they wore me down to break me and they did. I never understood the reason for the battle. I was never at fault, I was injured, and I paid insurance. We all know insurance does not like to pay out. So, I had a battle from hell on my hands and it took ten years of my life.

We moved into an exceptionally large house with a lot of land. Our Neighbors were the best you could ask for. I stayed home and took care of the house yard and other stuff wives do. There were beautiful rock gardens I brought back to life. There were fruit trees everywhere, apples, cherries, grapes, blueberries, raspberry, pears, and plums. All the fruit you ever wanted and at a great price, free. I had only one problem the house would be covered with spiders. I lost the freezing weather to gain spiders. I have never seen so many distinct kinds. We would kill about 20 and the next morning it would be covered again. There would be dock spiders in the house the size of a fifty-cent piece. The little black ones would bite and make you sick for days. I was starting to wish for mosquitos again.

We would find kids in our yard looking for the famous hallucinating magic mushrooms that grew wild on the property. I never did find out which ones they were. We ended up living there for a few months when my son decided to come out. Unfortunately, it didn't last. An issue with not getting a job and living on welfare. That never stood right with me. He did not want to cut his long hair to get a job. The priorities were demented. He needed to grow up and take on responsibilities. The final limit was when he bought a car with welfare money and had no license. Made no sense. He explained his father owed him money and he decided to buy the car with it. That did not sit well with peter and the next morning my son left. Once again, the relationship was severed. It did not matter what I did, my children continued to treat me poorly. I guess after a while it numbs you, you stop fighting it and jump into acceptance and move on with your life.

It was a matter of a few months before I would be asked if I would live on a boat. A boat? Are you kidding me? My greatest fear in life is water. I was petrified of water and now I was asked if I would face my fear. I did cave and we moved onto a 24ft Bay liner with just a two- burner stove, bar fridge and a toilet and sink. Easy to clean. Wow! The sacrifice from a three-bedroom house to a closet. You must be quite the woman to not only live on water but a cubby hole too. Against my better judgement which happened a lot in my life, I agreed to try it. There was no TV, but the boat needed work, so I did all the fixing up. The painting anything to bring the poorly treated vessel back up to standards. I loved that kind of work, and it was rewarding. We decided due to the lack of activity to my brain while not having my career, I would take courses at home. I began with Interior Decorating & Design. It would advance criminal law real estate to Adult Psychology down to Pet Grooming. I'm a Gemini and we thrive on knowledge and intelligent conversation. I need lots of input to survive. To hold conversations on any subject and hold my own. I continued to Business Management to Forensic Science and Private Investigating and finally ended with the only course I did not complete which was Creative Writing. I supported 100% on most and 89% on others. Keep my brain alive, it surely did.

One night we finally discussed marriage and set a date for June 28, 1998. It was held outside at the Marina in Maple Bay British, Columbia, Canada. There was already a bar and restaurant so it was all arranged that the reception would be held there, and the food prepared there as well. The forecast was rain but for the grace of God it started after the ceremony. The best part was Peter's mom Rita was going to be there and like a trooper, she slept on the couch in the boat with us. Crowded? Surprisingly not? She was a tiny woman. The wedding went well, and the best man decided he would sleep on our aft deck. Drunk he was walking down the dock when he walked right off the dock. All we heard was a huge splash and he was gone. Now afraid of water as I was, the worst thing that could happen to me is to end up in an ocean with octopuses, otters, crabs, and seals swimming around. I think I will pass.

It was a few months later when he arrived home and mentioned a boat on a hill that was for sale. A 47 ½ ft boat called an All West. He wanted me to look at it. When we arrived, it looked like a bus. Without hesitation I said I am not living in the ugly thing. He asked if I would humor him and look inside. It was a dump. Then I saw the four burner stove cupboards everywhere, larger fridge, toilet sink and shower. I was hooked. I would take that boat and turn it into a spectacular home with my decorating. The space was remarkable. Things were looking up. In the years to come we will redesign the entire boat. The command bridge was removed and the pilot house to make room for a forward birth. It was all done in pine with a black accent and the lighting down low. Eventually a tub was installed full fridge and an actual couch. It was stunning. Prior to redesigning we had named her The Joan B after my mom, but after it was redone, it became Thunderbolt. I did most of the decorating and my fair share of the labor. It was well worth it.

We would remain on that boat from 1998-2002. I had grown tired of the water and wanted a slide out trailer. The boat went up for sale and my lawsuit settled for peanuts. We moved to a place called the Living Forest in Nanaimo, B.C. I was in heaven campfires every night if there were no forest fires. Walking trails the water close buy and there were 1050 diverse types of birds. That is when I was really introduced to slugs and frogs who turned color to protect themselves. Prior to moving there and affording it to, I finally gave up and settled my lawsuit we had to go to Winnipeg, Manitoba Canada to face the insurance company's lawyer. Stressful but the support of Rita and my daughter was overwhelming. I had the immense joy of meeting three of my grandchildren for the first time. Unfortunately, I ended up with bronchial pneumonia and tried to keep my distance. Mom would join us back in B.C. and stay for a couple of weeks.

At that time, my brother was living here at the marina only in the trailer park. We financed a small trailer for him because he was living on the boat. It was not the greatest, so I decided to redo the entire inside of the trailer. Steve tried to help with the painting, his complaining was driving me to drink so I fired him. When it was complete, he presented me with a store-bought certificate where he could put what he wanted on it. It was special until the relationship soured once again. I had not seen him for decades just to watch the same pattern repeat itself. Why can't things be better? It soured after getting him a bigger trailer that would cost 7,000.00. We helped him do it and I am afraid to say he neglected to pay abandoned it while I had no key. And I lost 7,000.00 because my husband allowed him to put the trailer in his name instead of ours. Knowing my brother's history, I told him not to do it. Thanks, brother. He moved on and I would not hear from him for another five years let alone see him. The damage was done, and I did have to claim bankruptcy. His response, they were already in trouble, not I am sorry. This is my blood, my brother I looked up to, and then down too. I was not his target; it was all of us. At one time or another he has ruined our siblings' lives.

Looking back on my first book, I told you about the story of my grandfather who was going to rob the Fergus, Ontario, Canada's Bank. Now because of that my brother feels that it is hereditary so he comes by it honestly. Not exactly the word I would use. It would be the last time he would ever get any help from me. The relationship severed again. It did not bother me that the relationship was on the rocks. It is something I have been forced to learn to live with. Sometimes you just must accept this is who he is. He must want to change and he is not ready yet. Take your time bro! I will not be waiting for that miracle.

We left B.C. and never looked back. Peter got a trucking job and my daughter, and I were reunited, onto a new chapter. It lasted about a month. I decided to go trucking. I was staying with my daughter and things were tense, so I packed up and went off on a new adventure. I have always loved semis so trucking gave me another fascinating industry to feed knowledge from. I did it for fours when I decided I needed a place to live, have the grandchildren visit and stay on weekends. I wanted more. Soon I would get tired and just for a laugh I applied at Walmart and was hired at once. I stayed two years before moving onto Home Depot as an interior designer. The pay was great, and we bought our first house. It was a fixer her upper. I re-sanded the hardware floors, stucco the ceiling, put up wallpaper in the dining room and bedroom, painted. I quit work to concentrate on the house. We paid 60.000.00.

The relationship was great until a hot summer's night, June 12, 2009, my entire world would change. It started with a phone call. We had bought our own semi and the plan was we would make a million dollars retire and then lease out our truck. Financially we would be set to retire comfortably, but someone had other plans for us. A man decided he was going to commit suicide by semi. He came clear across the highway and crashed into our rig. Peter had a load on so he tried to back up as much as he could without the product coming through the back window. But it was not enough, and the car took the front of the semi completely off. His career and our dreams were shattered that day, but what would happen over the next thirteen years would bring this marriage to its knees. The battle with the same insurance I had would now become his. I fought my fought, now it was his turn. I was bitter with my dealings, but I was not prepared for them to steal my dignity, my spirit and my trust in people; he on the other hand became enraged, bitter and plain mean.

The world became his enemy, he allowed them to take away the best parts of him. The anger consumed him. What you believed this was personal, look around, we all have been abused by the system, get over it and make whatever you have left and survive. I could really understand it if his injuries crippled him, but it didn't any more than it did mine. Move on! No matter how hard I tried to help and understand, he would cast me aside. It was not long before he decided he did not want to live in Winnipeg. The house we bought was a steppingstone, one he had no intention of keeping. A small town was what he wanted. Grandview, Manitoba where we had other property, we had bought prior but no help organizing all contractors. When do they say small towns are relaxed? This town took it to the extreme. No return phone calls, which left me confused why they were running a business, I know what you are thinking? Maybe they are busy? Everyone loves getting messages, they do not check. Odd?

He was not backing down and a move in his mind was his rescue, in my mind, it was sadness. I would be leaving behind my children again, only this time my grandchildren. It was clear his side of the family was not as important as mine to me. We had chosen that house mainly because the grandchildren were two blocks away, and now I was leaving again, but not without the reassurance that they would visit in the summer. Our Granddaughter delaney was the most hurt by the news. I pushed in the sadness and the pain of being so far away. I have just re-united with my children and off I go again doing what I do best, please their spouse. Do not get me wrong, I did not like Winnipeg, but Grandview was too small. Population 804 hundred people. Like living on a cul-de-sac where all your neighbors know you, and your business no matter how guarded you are. The house on Johnson was bought for 60,000.00. I spent my time renovating the house to suit my needs. I was able to go in early and re-do the hardwood flooring, painting all the rooms and making it suitable. It was my second hand at decorating and taking something ugly like boats and turning it into a piece of art if you will? Stuccoing and wallpaper added a nice touch.

We found the house in Grandview. Asking price 45,000.00. Take one look and we offered

28,000.00 take it or leave it. They took the offer and now it was my time to shine. To turn another deluge wreck into a mansion. I was in for the challenge. There I was packing again. I spent my entire life between my career and marriages packing. My new adventure was about to begin.

CHAPTER
ELEVEN

There would be one thing great though, we managed to get the bedroom painted, the kitchen flooring and carpet in the bedroom done prior to the move. I knew I would feel the loss of my children and grandchildren, but I knew my mind would be in mandated with ideas for the new house. My life would become hectic and would continue until everything was complete. Everything was trashed in the bathroom and started from nothing. New flooring everywhere, all the walls to be painted and worst of all, wallpaper removed. I was extremely lucky it was dry strippable it would take four coats of primer and three of paint. What attracted me was the molding in the house. I was able to contrast colors. Kitchen cupboards were to the point of being bleached before I could apply paint. It would take months to get the old girl looking beautiful again. The outside of the house would be next. When it was completed, it was not bad for a two-bedroom bungalow.

Now 28,000.00 doesn't get you a great deal. The basement was a problem, it leaked. We contacted a contractor to fix it and never showed up. Amazing it was a repeat of lack of interest when I lived in Winnipeg. Laid back? Or lazy? So, it was never completed. For a few years it seemed fine, then in a heartbeat it was flooding. Once again, we approached a company to have it repaired and once again no one showed up. Frustrated, we just completely blocked it from our minds and decided on a quick fix. Never go that route unless you can manage to waste material along with your money. The house was now completely done in the inside and freshly painted on the outside, I became bored and decided to get a job at the local store, in short.... That did not last long.

There was no employment there. Goes with the territory of small towns.

It was not long before I seen the town inundated with small dogs. I thought to myself, we need a groomer in town. Took to the studies on Animal Science and Pet Grooming. After the courses I put the knowledge to work and started Joey's Professional Grooming. I now own my own business. I am an intelligent woman who always perceived myself as knowledgeable as the people I worked for or under. I would now become my own boss; the freedom was unbelievable. Work when I wanted to. I was excited and was looking forward to my first client. I had two small dogs myself and did not realize when I rescued them, they grew hair like no tomorrow. I had Benji and Toby my new friends and guinea pigs. I enjoyed meeting the town's dogs and becoming an important person in their lives. Soon it became clear that we needed to build my own shop. It turned out beautiful. Before I knew I had clients eager to have their dogs done. It wasn't a money busting amount, but it covered enough of the bills. I really enjoyed but after Seven years my Fibromyalgia was progressing and became debilitating.

Then came the time to remodel the kitchen. It was an older home, so the cupboards were too small. The dining room was dismantled, and a beam was installed. It became massive. I decided to put a fireplace on the feature wall with brick behind it. I was amazed at how beautiful the kitchen looked and most of the labor was done by me. The house was re-appraised from 45,000.00-65,000.00 upon completion. I decided to make a tire garden surrounded by limestone rocks with a border of white rocks. Statues were placed and the garden tires were filled with flowers. The yard was massive, so something had to be done. A fence soon followed. Many years later I would plant spruce trees to help fill the empty spaces. The first house you see when entering Grandview, so I felt obligated, or my duty to help represent the town.

We added a sundeck and a garage for my 2016 Camaro Convertible. It would be stored every winter which kept the mileage down on my vehicle. Great for resale and in fact it did just that. I would soon become bored and would need outside stimulation, so I went back to work. My marriage was moving backwards and arguments insued, tempers flaring, I needed an escape. I started working as a caregiver, but funny I should end up needing the same in a few years. At first, I was having difficulty with the entire system, but I stuck with it and did an amazing job. When I was at work, I was happy, content, but when I walked through my door after a long shift, it just did not feel like home anymore. Soon I found myself at work more than home. The company hired people who did not like coming to work, or phoning in sick. Never have I seen anything like that before. I gave the company one and half years before I tired of the poor management.

CHAPTER
TWELVE

It was a beautiful spring day when I awoke and knew there was something different with me. I was covered in sweat, head pounding with excruciating pain and too weak to move. After resting awhile, I decided to mow the lawn. I walked approximately twenty steps when I couldn't do it anymore. I returned to the house to lay down. When supper was ready, I could only eat three bites and felt sick. I could not consume liquids. I dealt with this along with the arguments of not eating with my ex for two months, dropping in weight drastically twenty-eight IBS in a month. I could not function as I watched my house turn into a filthy shack, but there was no energy left in me. It was time to see the doctor.

I was sent for a C T SCAN, and they found nothing. So, I approached another doctor, she in turn sent me for a Scan this time with dye. The results were in five days later. The longest days of my life. The weekend came and no news is good news, maybe just the flu. Monday morning rolled around when the call came in for me to come to the clinic at once. The fear began to set in. I looked at my ex and waited to hear he would be joining me. Isn't that what couples do? I arrived and was directed into my doctor's office and waited patiently, no, I did not. She sat beside me and told me I had a tumor tucked deep into my lung and extremely close to my heart. This is bad, she would tell me. It is almost two inches long, I had cancer. What did you just say? Cancer? She then told me she would see that I saw one of the best Thoracic Surgeons. She kept that promise. She then told me how sorry she was. I left in a daze, confused, I quit smoking twenty-three years ago, how can this be? I quit repairing my lungs so I would not get cancer! What a kick in the head!

I walked through the door, and I looked him square in the face and said I had cancer and walked out of the room. I needed to compose myself. I then returned and told him now do you understand why I could not eat and yelling at me was not going to correct this problem. Then the words that came from his mouth edged inside my brain forever. Why is this happening to me? What? Happening to you? Wow! If there was any love left in that marriage, yes, you guessed it, it was drained from my tired and restless body. Somehow, I realized, I was now on my own. How alone I became is the next part of this series. I would become so sick I could not move. Gobbling Tylenol 3's to try and keep the headaches at bay, sleeping from a soaked bed to a soaked couch back and forth all night. Now I have lost forty-five LBS. When finally, a satellite conference with my new Surgeon Dr Tan approached. We went through the symptoms by him asking questions. I knew at that moment; I had cancer, and it was serious. There will be the movie C T SCANS and finally a P. E. T Scan. Unfortunately, it didn't show much so they ordered a biopsy for December2021.

I would need to travel to Winnipeg again. I stayed with my younger sister Sherri and her husband Richard. They took diligent care of me while I was there. Then the biopsy was completed and now to find out if it is not Benine. I had cancer and would need major surgery. My beautiful niece angel was present when I met with the surgeon for support. That is when he informed me by operation is a dangerous one. The tumor being stuck into my lung and near the heart made it a difficult surgery, my odds were not great, chances where I was not getting off that table. He would repeatedly tell me my odds to try and make sure I understood the dangers of this operation. I had to fully understand the risks, and I did. The alternative would be to just suffer and let it multiply until I die. No, book me please. Surgery was scheduled for April 8, 2022. I would once again face another surgery alone. I managed to stay with my daughter Shannon for a couple of days and we were estranged for a while, so it was great seeing her. My ex picked me up and expected me to carry my suitcase down the three flights of stairs after a biopsy was performed on my chest. I was in shock, for the lack of caring was nonexistent. Wow! It was a four-hour drive and all he did was raise his voice at me until we got to our doorstep. I am fighting a losing battle in every aspect of my life, and it was not about to change.

Christmas came and I had no desire for it. My world was crashing around me. I was existing instead of living, trapped in a marriage gone horribly wrong and cancer to fight. I had no fight left in me, my strength gone only weakness. I wonder why me? My life has been one roller coaster ride after another, why haven't the wheels fallen off the track?

Someone please help me off. The only help available was coming directly from me. There was no medicine I could take, I would have to endure living this nightmare a year before the surgery, but grateful at the same time, there were others far worse than I and it saddens me. Decade after decade people support the cancer society, but there is no cure. They said that 24% of people in Manitoba with lung cancer will die by the end of this year. Why can't we help them? To stop this debilitating disease. It is heart breaking.

I found myself sinking into deep depression with no one to relate to, to talk to. I was alone. Strange that I would come this far in life to remain as I was a book ago. Loneliness has become my only friend, so I decided to make a change. The battle brewing in the household was getting too old and my stress level was sky rocketing. Walking on eggshells, I did not even want to be in the same room anymore. I could feel, my love, my heart, my understanding and caring dissipate into thin air and hatred begin to take control, followed with disgust. There was nothing left, gone, thirty years wasted and turned into such contempt for each other. Now, I am sure he would disagree with most of this, but in all fairness, I was left to deal with and try to cure my cancer alone. So, I decided, the screaming would stop, the silence between us would stop, the love had vanished, and the respect deteriorated the relationship to its ruins. Time for me to move on. To find any form of happiness if it exists and at my age, would I finally get to embrace it. True love and happiness. I haven't seen it in my life yet. Is it waiting for me around some corner, searching and reaching for me? I did not know the answer to the questions, but I was not going to stop searching for it either.

It would happen that there would be someone and a few more to follow. The roller coaster ride I have been losing control over would collide in a way that no one could ever have imagined. The destruction and devastation that follows will make your heart sink and your blood kurl. Your faith in humanity questioned, your love destroyed, ill repair to your trust and have you pull the reins on your heart and remove it to a safe and hidden place. To have no control of your life. You have become nothing, insignificantly unimportant and mentally beaten.

You my friends and fellow readers, yes book three is imminent and will be available in the very near future.